This 90 Day New Testament Bible Reading Plan Belongs To:

_____

{ Christina & Jodi }
HAND-DESIGNED FOR HIS GLORY!

Our Story
Two friends coming together by living as neighbors, raising our children and keeping our family connected as we all grow in Christ.

With our inspirational journals, planners, coloring books and bible reading plans, we hope to encourage and bless others through these self hand-designed art books to strengthen one another in **His glory!**

Copyright © 2019 Christina & Jodi
All rights reserved.
No part of this book may be reproduced or redistributed without express permission from the author and publishing company. Licensed graphics used with all appropriate commercial licenses.

Day 1
Read Matthew 1-3

Notes

Encourage one another and build each other up

Day 2
Read Matthew 4-6

Notes

> BE STRONG IN THE **LORD** AND IN THE **POWER** OF HIS MIGHT
> EPHESIANS 6:10

Day 3
Read Matthew 7-9

Notes

Jesus is the light in a darken world

Day 4
Read Matthew 10-12

Notes

as the deer longs for streams of water so i long for you O God

Psalm 42:1

Day 5
Read Matthew 13-15

Notes

Day 6
Read Matthew 16-18

Notes

Day 7
Read Matthew 19-21

Notes

Love never fails
1 CORINTHIANS 13:8

Day 8
Read Matthew 22-24

Notes

For We walk By Faith Not By Sight
2 CORINTHIANS 5:7

Day 9
Read Matthew 25-26

Notes

it is well with my Soul

Day 10
Read Matthew 27-28

Notes

Day 11
Read Mark 1-3

Notes

Encourage one another and build each other up

Day 12
Read Mark 4-5

Notes

> **BE STRONG IN THE LORD AND IN THE POWER OF HIS MIGHT**
> EPHESIANS 6:10

Day 13
Read Mark 6-8

Notes

Jesus is the light in a darken world

Day 14
Read Mark 9-11

Notes

as the deer longs for streams of water so i long for you O God

Psalm 42:1

Day 15
Read Mark 12-14

Notes

Day 16
Read Mark 15-16

Notes

Sunshine and Jesus

Day 17
Read Luke 1-2

Notes

Day 18
Read Luke 3-5

Notes

For We walk By Faith Not By Sight
2 CORINTHIANS 5:7

Day 19
Read Luke 6-8

Notes

it is well with my Soul

Day 20
Read Luke 9-10

Notes

Day 21
Read Luke 11-13

Notes

Encourage one another and build each other up

Day 22
Read Luke 14-16

Notes

> BE STRONG IN THE **LORD** AND IN THE **POWER** OF HIS MIGHT
> EPHESIANS 6:10

Day 23
Read Luke 17-18

Notes

Jesus is the light in a darken world

Day 24
Read Luke 19-20

Notes

as the deer longs for streams of water so i long for you O God

Psalm 42:1

Day 25
Read Luke 21-22

Notes

Day 26
Read Luke 23-24

Notes

Day 27
Read John 1-2

Notes

Day 28
Read John 3-5

Notes

For We walk By Faith Not By Sight

2 CORINTHIANS 5:7

Day 29
Read John 6-8

Notes

it is well with my Soul

Day 30
Read John 9-11

Notes

> I CAN DO ALL THINGS THROUGH Christ WHO GIVES ME STRENGTH
> · PHILIPPIANS 4:13 ·

Day 31
Read John 12-13

Notes

Encourage one another and BUILD each other up

Day 32
Read John 14-16

Notes

Day 33
Read John 17-19

Notes

Jesus is the light in a darken world

Day 34
Read John 20-21

Notes

as the deer longs for streams of water so i long for you O God

Psalm 42:1

Day 35
Read Acts 1-2

Notes

Day 36
Read Acts 3-5

Notes

Day 37
Read Acts 6-7

Notes

Day 38
Read Acts 8-9

Notes

For we walk by faith not by sight
2 CORINTHIANS 5:7

Day 39
Read Acts 10-11

Notes

Day 40
Read Acts 12-14

Notes

Day 41
Read Acts 15-16

Notes

Encourage one another and build each other up

Day 42
Read Acts 17-18

Notes

> BE STRONG IN THE **LORD** AND IN THE **POWER** OF HIS MIGHT
> EPHESIANS 6:10

Day 43
Read Acts 19-21

Notes

Jesus is the light in a darken world

Day 44
Read Acts 22-23

Notes

as the deer longs for streams of water so i long for you O God

Psalm 42:1

Day 45
Read Acts 24-25

Notes

Day 46
Read Acts 26-28

Notes

Day 47
Read Romans 1-3

Notes

Love never fails
I Corinthians 13:8

Day 48
Read Romans 4-6

Notes

For we walk by faith, not by sight
2 CORINTHIANS 5:7

Day 49
Read Romans 7-8

Notes

it is well with my Soul

Day 50
Read Romans 9-10

Notes

Day 51
Read Romans 11-13

Notes

Encourage one another and build each other up

Day 52
Read Romans 14-16

Notes

> BE STRONG IN THE **LORD** AND IN THE **POWER** OF HIS MIGHT
> EPHESIANS 6:10

Day 53
Read 1 Corinthians 1-3

Notes

Day 54
Read 1 Corinthians 4-6

Notes

as the deer longs for streams of water so i long for you O God

Psalm 42:1

Day 55
Read 1 Corinthians 7-9

Notes

Day 56
Read 1 Corinthians 10-11

Notes

Day 57
Read 1 Corinthians 12-14

Notes

Love never fails
1 Corinthians 13:8

Day 58
Read 1 Corinthians 15-16

Notes

For we walk by faith not by sight
2 CORINTHIANS 5:7

Day 59

Read 2 Corinthians 1-3

Notes

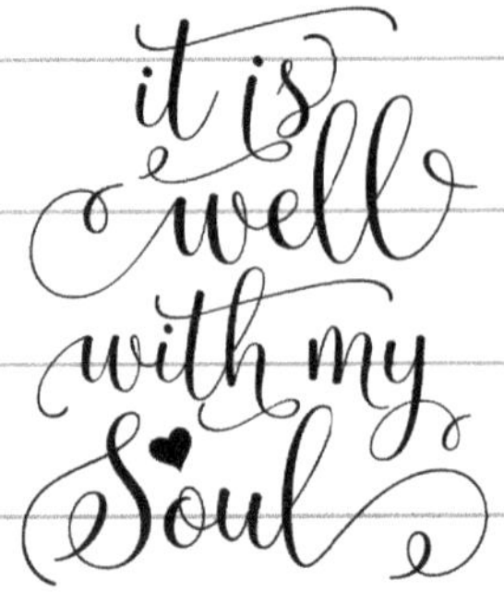
it is well with my Soul

Day 60
Read 2 Corinthians 4-7

Notes

Day 61
Read 2 Corinthians 8-10

Notes

Encourage one another and build each other up

Day 62
Read 2 Corinthians 11-13

Notes

> BE STRONG IN THE LORD AND IN THE POWER OF HIS MIGHT
> EPHESIANS 6:10

Day 63
Read Galatians 1-3

Notes

Jesus is the light in a darken world

Day 64
Read Galatians 4-6

Notes

as the deer longs for streams of water so I long for you O God

Psalm 42:1

Day 65
Read Ephesians 1-3

Notes

Day 66
Read Ephesians 4-6

Notes

Day 67
Read Philippians

Notes

Day 68
Read Colossians

Notes

For We walk By Faith Not By Sight
2 CORINTHIANS 5:7

Day 69
Read 1 Thessalonians

Notes

it is well with my Soul

Day 70
Read 2 Thessalonians

Notes

Day 71
Read 1 Timothy 1-3

Notes

Encourage one another and build each other up

Day 72
Read 1 Timothy 4-6

Notes

> BE STRONG IN THE LORD AND IN THE POWER OF HIS MIGHT
> EPHESIANS 6:10

Day 73
Read 2 Timothy

Notes

Jesus is the light in a darken world

Day 74
Read Titus & Philemon

Notes

as the deer longs for streams of water so i long for you O God

Psalm 42:1

Day 75

Read Hebrews 1-3

Notes

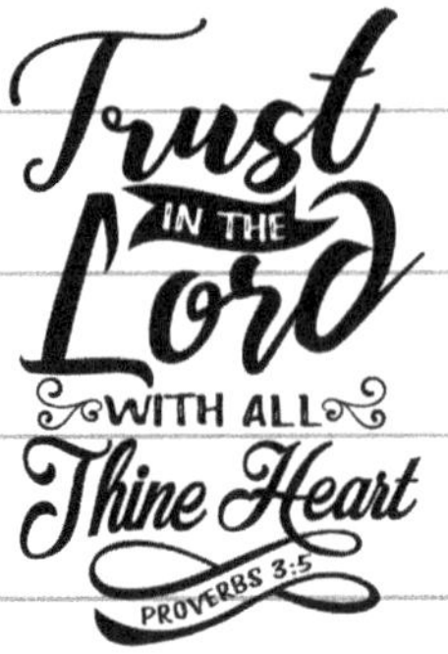

Day 76
Read Hebrews 4-6

Notes

Day 77
Read Hebrews 7-10

Notes

Day 78
Read Hebrews 11-13

Notes

For we walk by faith, not by sight.
2 CORINTHIANS 5:7

Day 79
Read James

Notes

Day 80
Read 1 Peter

Notes

Day 81
Read 2 Peter

Notes

Encourage one another and build each other up

Day 82
Read 1 John

Notes

> BE STRONG IN THE LORD AND IN THE POWER OF HIS MIGHT
> EPHESIANS 6:10

Day 83
Read 2 & 3 John

Notes

Day 84
Read Revelation 1-3

Notes

as the deer longs for streams of water so i long for you O God

Psalm 42:1

Day 85
Read Revelation 4-7

Notes

Day 86
Read Revelation 8-10

Notes

Day 87
Read Revelation 11-13

Notes

Day 88
Read Revelation 14-16

Notes

For We walk By Faith Not By Sight
2 CORINTHIANS 5:7

Day 89
Read Revelation 17-19

Notes

Day 90
Read Revelation 20-22

Notes

You Did It Congratulations!

Notes

Encourage one another and BUILD each other up

www.ingramcontent.com/pod-product-compliance
Lightning Source LLC
LaVergne TN
LVHW051700020125
800322LV00002B/248